A Daily
Journaling
and
Meditation System

BRAIN DUMP

LINDA PAOLUCCIO

BALBOA

Balboa Press books may be ordered through booksellers or by contacting:

Balboa Press
A Division of Hay House
1663 Liberty Drive
Bloomington, IN 47403
www.balboapress.com
1 (877) 407-4847

ISBN: 978-1-5043-2566-0 (sc)
ISBN: 978-1-5043-2567-7 (e)

Library of Congress Control Number: 2014922631

Print information available on the last page.

Balboa Press rev. date: 02/19/2015

Welcome to The Brain Dump Journaling System

Volume 1 – Peeling the Onion in New Recovery

Most mediation journal formats include a daily directive or something to consider. Brain Dump is different. Rather than give you something to think about or reflect on, we want you to learn about what *you* are thinking about. It is a design to assist you in discovering your true nature. The goal is to discover who you really are, what you really want, and what is really going on in your own mind. In actively pursuing your own mind, you will find out what motivates you, what is causing stress, fear, or other barriers to progress, or perhaps thinking that is leading you to relapse.

As you practice this method, you are developing the new patterns of self- discipline and emotional regulation that are necessary for long term sobriety.

Did you know that the average person has somewhere between 50,000 and 70,000 thoughts each and everyday? And, that we are only actually conscious of about 5%? (LONI, 2014) That's crazy, right?

Most of our actions and behaviors begin with thoughts, both conscious and unconscious thoughts SO... It makes sense to *notice* what you are thinking about, ***RIGHT?***

One of the best ways to do this is meditation. You might think, "Yikes! Meditation? I can't do that, my mind just races!" *that is exactly the point!*

Brain Dump is a daily practice that will assist you in several aspects of your daily life:

- ❖ You will notice a new sense of calm and control of your mental and emotional states.
- ❖ You will become more aware of what is going on in your own mind and determine who is driving this bus anyway?
- ❖ You will receive answers to questions like: *Who am I? What do I really want? How do I feel?*

Through this practice, you will be in better control of your feelings **and** gain ability to change unwanted behaviors... People who have used this practice for 30 days or longer report:

- ❖ Better focus
- ❖ Mood improvement
- ❖ Improved of self-esteem
- ❖ Better sleep
- ❖ Balance
- ❖ Emotional Regulation
- ❖ A host of other benefits that may help you with your sobriety!

Whether you are stressed, in fear, experience relapse or other negative results, you may not even realize the truth of why you are suffering ... we cannot change what we cannot see, right? So it makes perfect sense to pay a little attention to what your own mind is telling you!

Ready to give it a try? Great! Lets get started!

At the beginning of each day you will get up, use the bathroom, grab your coffee (or what ever you like to drink) and go your quiet place (if you don't have one, create one) where you will not be disturbed for at least a half hour, yes at least a half hour. This may mean that you have to get up earlier than others in your household, but trust me; you *will* learn to love this practice. This is truly taking care of *you* and you will soon realize that it is assisting you in becoming who you want to be.

Every two weeks we will introduce a new concept to your daily process to assist you on your journey.

You can continue your journey with The Brain Dump Journal System.

Look for future volumes addressing more issues such as romance, finance, and career/occupation.

☮

Day 1

We will first start with a very short "meditation", but rather than try and "still" your mind – The idea is to **Notice it**...yes, notice what you are thinking about, *without* judgment if you can. (Don't worry, this will get easier every day)

Begin by sitting quietly for about 5 minutes.

Sitting up straight, no leaning back on the chair, just you, holding you up. Now breathe in through your nose and out through your mouth. Count your breaths, 1 inhale, 2 exhale, 3 inhale, 4 exhale and so on... until you reach 10. Repeat this until you feel a little more relaxed, probably a few rounds of 10. Once you feel somewhat relaxed and with your eyes closed and in a semi-relaxed state, begin to notice what your mind does... try and catch a thought. Do this for a few minutes. Close your eyes and relax.

Breathe. Let the thoughts come, and without judgment, let them go.

After about 5 minutes (it may not seem like a long time until you actually try it, then it may feel like forever! Consistency is most important to receive results! Stick with it!!!) notice if there are dominant thoughts... is there something that just keeps coming up for you? Catch a thought and write it down and then begin writing freely.

Write furiously for 10 minutes:

Feelin a little stuck? Ok, so here are some questions to assist you... Don't worry you'll find your flow, just keep going!

1) What did you notice?

_____

_____

2) How do you feel right now?

_____

_____

3) Are you anxious? Why or what about?

_____

_____

4) How much of what you were thinking is meaningful?

_____

_____

Keep going! Dump!!!

_____

_____

_____

☮

_____

_____

_____

_____

_____

_____

_____

_____

_____

_____

_____

_____

_____

_____

_____

Now that you have removed some of the thoughts that clutter up your mind, try to sit for a moment or two and design your day. You may wish to return to the thought that you caught and decide if it is something important or if it is a fear or? If it is something that will serve you, then write about it. What attention does it need? After you have completed this it is time to design your day:

1) What is most important for me today?

_____

_____

2) What do I need to do?

_____

_____

3) What are my goals for the day?

_____

_____

4) Who do I want to be today?

_____

_____

5) What do I need today?

_____

_____

Day 2

Welcome back! Be patient with yourself and with this. There is a good chance that you may fight this a little... Don't worry, this is natural and it's a great opportunity to notice how your thoughts are affecting your behavior. It may be tempting to put it off, or to tell yourself that you will do "it" later but this is exactly where you push through! Do it!!! Ok, ready? Begin by sitting quietly. Now breathe in 1, breathe out 2, in 3, out 4... relax. Breathe. Notice what your mind is doing. Is it mocking you? What stories is it telling you? Is it full of "shoulds"? Is it making fun of this practice or trying to sabotage your progress? Relax, breathe and just notice; don't judge. Just notice and accept that your mind is doing it's job; thinking. Relax, it will get easier.

After you have finished your "noticing meditation", catch a thought and write it down. Then dump all of the surrounding thoughts that don't serve you. Get rid of it! Write.

_____

_____

_____

_____

_____

_____

_____

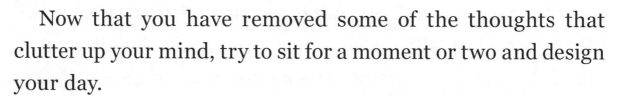

_____

_____

_____

_____

_____

Now that you have removed some of the thoughts that clutter up your mind, try to sit for a moment or two and design your day.

You *may* wish to return to the thought that you caught and decide if it is something important or if it is a fear or...? If it is something that will serve you, then write about it. What attention does it need? After you have completed this it is time to **design** your day:

1) What is most important for me today?

_____

_____

2) What do I need to do?

_____

_____

☮

3) What are my goals for the day?

_____

_____

4) Who do I want to be today?

_____

_____

5) What do I need today?

_____

_____

Day 3 – Yeay! You're on your way to a great new life! Keep going!

Sit quietly. Breathe in 1, breathe out 2, in 3, out 4... relax. Breathe. Notice what your mind is doing. Is it messing with you? Is it telling you stupid things? Is it full of "what if's" ? Is it making fun of this practice or trying to sabotage your progress? Just chill, breathe and notice; don't judge. Just notice and accept that your mind is doing it's job; thinking.

After you have finished your "noticing meditation", catch a thought and write it down. Then dump all of the surrounding thoughts that don't serve you. Dump it! Write.

_____

_____

_____

_____

_____

_____

_____

_____

_____

_____

Ok, now that you have removed some of the thoughts that clutter up your mind, try to sit for a moment or two and design your day.

You may wish to return to the thought that you caught and decide if it is something important or if it is a fear or? If it is something that will serve you, then write it out. What attention does it need? After you have completed this it is time to design your day:

1) What is most important for me today?

_____

_____

2) What do I need to do?

_____

_____

3) What are my goals for the day?

_____

_____

4) Who do I want to be today?

_____

_____

5) What do I need today?

_____

_____

Day 4 – This is gonna pay off, don't quit!

Sit quietly. Breathe in 1, breathe out 2, in 3, out 4... relax. Breathe. Notice what your mind is doing. Is it mocking you? What stories is it telling you? Is it full of "shoulds" ? is it making fun of this practice or trying to sabotage your progress? Relax, breathe and just notice; don't judge. Just notice and accept that your mind is doing it's job; thinking.

After you have finished your "noticing meditation", catch a thought and write it down. Then dump all of the surrounding thoughts that don't serve you. Write.

_____

_____

_____

_____

_____

_____

_____

_____

_____

_____

_____

☮

Now that you have removed some of the thoughts that clutter up your mind, try to sit for a moment or two and design your day.

You may wish to return to the thought that you caught and decide if it is something important or if it is a fear or? If it is something that will serve you, then write about it. What attention does it need? After you have completed this it is time to design your day:

1) What is most important for me today?

_____

_____

2) What do I need to do?

_____

_____

3) What are my goals for the day?

_____

_____

4) Who do I want to be today?

_____

_____

5) What do I need today?

_____

_____

Day 5 – Keep going! You're doing great! Repetition is part of the deal...push through, notice what stories your head is telling you... Read each word, there are subtle changes that you don't want to miss...What are you beginning to see about how your mind will try to sway you?

Ok now, you know the drill...Sit quietly. Breathe in 1, breathe out 2, in 3, out 4... relax. Breathe. Breathe. Breathe. Notice what your mind is doing. Is it mocking you? What stories is it telling you? Is it full of "shoulds" ? What is it making fun of? Who is it criticizing? How has it trying to sabotage your progress? Relax, breathe and just notice; don't judge. Just notice and accept that your mind is doing it's job; thinking.

After you have finished your "noticing meditation", catch a thought and write it down. Then dump all of the surrounding thoughts that don't serve you. Write.

_____

_____

_____

_____

_____

_____

_____

_____

☮

_____

_____

_____

_____

_____

Now that you have removed some of the thoughts that clutter up your mind, try to sit for a moment or two and design your day.

You may wish to return to the thought that you caught and decide if it is something important or if it is a fear or? If it is something that will serve you, then write about it. What attention does it need? After you have completed this it is time to design your day:

1) What is most important for me today?

_____

_____

2) What do I need to do?

_____

_____

3) What are my goals for the day?

_____

_____

4) Who do I want to be today?

_____

_____

5) What do I need today?

_____

_____

Day 6 – Hello there, *you* have a brand new day; choose to *create* a good one!

Begin your practice as usual (you have a "usual" by now.) Sit quietly. Breathe in 1, breathe out 2, in 3, out 4... relax. Breathe. Notice what your mind is doing. Is it telling you to cut corners, or that you don't need this? What stories is it telling you? Is it full of "should-a would-a could-a's" ? Is it telling you that you don't have it as bad as others or trying to sabotage your progress? Relax, breathe and just notice; don't judge. Just notice and accept that your mind is doing it's job; thinking.

After you have finished your "noticing meditation", catch a thought and write it down. Then dump all of the surrounding thoughts that don't serve you. Write.

_____

_____

_____

_____

_____

_____

_____

_____

☮

_____

_____

_____

Now that you have removed some of the thoughts that clutter up your mind, try to sit for a moment or two and design your day.

You may wish to return to the thought that you caught and decide if it is something important or if it is a fear or? If it is something that will serve you, then write about it. What attention does it need? After you have completed this it is time to design your day:

1) What is most important for me today?

_____

_____

2) What do I need to do?

_____

_____

3) What are my goals for the day?

_____

_____

4) Who do I want to be today?

_____

_____

5) What do I need today?

_____

_____

Day 7 – Keep going! You're doing great!

This will be the end of your first week. How are you feeling? What kinds of things are you noticing? How is your focus? What kind of subtle changes happening? Ok then, ready? Start by sitting quietly. Now bring your focus to your breath. Breathing in 1, breathe out 2, in 3, out 4... relax. Breathe. Notice what your mind is doing. What do you notice today? What kind of stories is your head telling you? Is it full of___ ? Is it making fun of this you or others or... is it trying to sabotage your progress? Relax, breathe and just notice; *don't judge*. Just notice and accept that your mind is doing it's job; thinking.

After you have finished your "noticing meditation", catch a thought and write it down. Then dump all of the surrounding thoughts that don't serve you. Write it!

_____

_____

_____

_____

_____

_____

_____

_____

_____

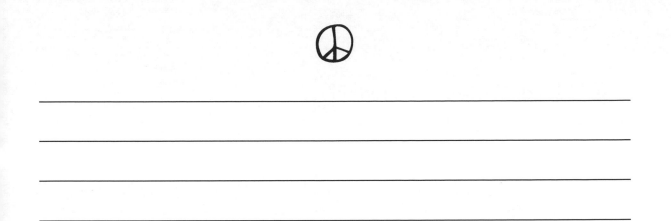

_____

_____

_____

_____

Now that you have seen and dumped some of the thoughts that clutter up your mind, try to sit for a moment or two and design your day.

You may wish to return to the thought that you caught and decide if it is something important or if it is a fear or? If it is something that will serve you, then write about it. What attention does it need? After you have completed this it is time to design your day:

1) What is most important for me today?

_____

_____

2) What do I need to do?

_____

_____

3) What are my goals for the day?

_____

_____

4) Who do I want to be today?

_____

_____

5) What do I need today?

_____

_____

Day 8 – Hey you! Yes you, you did it! You finished your first week!!! Way to go! Keep it up! Lets jam through week 2 and see where it leads you! Do this!!!

New recovery can be tough for some, and easier for others. There is no "one size fits all" so... You may be feeling more relaxed and notice that you love this new practice OR.... Things may be coming up for you that upset you, scare you or cause you pain... this might be a good opportunity to bring those concerns to your counselor or sponsor? Feelings, even the crappy ones, are natural and there is a solution! Never ever ever suffer in silence...reach out! Week 2 will be very much the same but you may add 1 or 2 minutes if you like to your meditation time.

Sit quietly. Breathe in 1, breathe out 2, in 3, out 4... relax. Breathe. Notice what your mind is doing. What messages is your head telling you? Notice, just notice and let the thoughts pass like clouds. Is it focused on something? Are there thoughts of using? Is it messin with you, trying to sabotage your progress? Relax, breathe and just notice; don't judge. Just notice and accept that your mind is doing it's job; thinking.

After you have finished your "noticing meditation", catch a thought and write it down. Then dump all of the surrounding thoughts that don't serve you. Write.

_____

_____

_____

_____

Now that you have removed some of the thoughts that clutter up your mind, try to sit for a moment or two and design your day.

You may wish to return to the thought that you caught and decide if it is something important or if it is a fear or? If it is something that will serve you, then write about it. What attention does it need? After you have completed this it is time to design your day. Remember, you can be what you chose:

1) What is most important for me today?

2) What do I need to do?

_____

_____

3) What are my goals for the day?

_____

_____

4) Who do I want to be today?

_____

_____

5) What do I need today?

_____

_____

Day 9 – Yeay, yeay yeay! Great job!

Sit quietly. **Take a moment to settle in and scan over your body and mind…Are you feeling happy? Excited? Tense? Stressed? Depressed? Relaxed? Notice it. Now that you have this awareness, it is up to you, really! Ready, begin…** Breathe in 1, breathe out 2, in 3, out 4… relax. Breathe. Notice what your mind is doing. Is it mocking you? What stories is it telling you? Is it full of "shoulds" ? is it making fun of this practice or trying to sabotage your progress? Relax, breathe and just notice; don't judge. Just notice and accept that your mind is doing it's job; thinking.

After you have finished your "noticing meditation", catch a thought and write it down. Then dump all of the surrounding thoughts that don't serve you. Write.

_____

_____

_____

_____

_____

_____

_____

_____

_____

_____

_____

_____

_____

Now that you have removed some of the thoughts that clutter up your mind, try to sit for a moment or two and design your day.

You may wish to return to the thought that you caught and decide if it is something important or if it is a fear or? If it is something that will serve you, then write about it. What attention does it need? After you have completed this it is time to design your day:

1) What is most important for me today?

_____

_____

2) What do I need to do?

_____

_____

3) What are my goals for the day?

_____

_____

☮

4) Who do I want to be today?

_____

_____

5) What do I need today?

_____

_____

Day 10 – Keep going! You're doing great!

Begin as per your usual. Relax. Notice how you are feeling. Sit quietly. Breathe in 1, breathe out 2, in 3, out 4… relax. Breathe. Notice what your mind is doing. Is it ready to begin? What stories is it telling you? Is it full of "shoulds" ? is it making fun of this practice or trying to sabotage your progress? Relax, breathe and just notice; don't judge. Just notice and accept that your mind is doing its job; thinking.

After you have finished your "noticing meditation", catch a thought and write it down. Then dump all of the surrounding thoughts that don't serve you. Write.

_____

_____

_____

_____

_____

_____

_____

_____

_____

_____

Now that you have removed some of the thoughts that clutter up your mind, try to sit for a moment or two and design your day.

You may wish to return to the thought that you caught and decide if it is something important or if it is a fear or? If it is something that will serve you, then write about it. What attention does it need? After you have completed this it is time to design your day:

1) What is most important for me today?

_____

_____

2) What do I need to do?

_____

_____

3) What are my goals for the day?

_____

_____

4) Who do I want to be today?

_____

_____

5) What do I need today?

_____

_____

Day 11 – You should be super proud of you!

Sit quietly. Breathe in 1, breathe out 2, in 3, out 4... relax. Breathe. Notice what your mind is doing. Is it mocking you? What stories is it telling you? Is it full of "shoulds" ? is it making fun of this practice or trying to sabotage your progress? Relax, breathe and just notice; don't judge. Just notice and accept that your mind is doing it's job; thinking.

After you have finished your "noticing meditation", catch a thought and write it down. Then dump all of the surrounding thoughts that don't serve you. Write.

_____

_____

_____

_____

_____

_____

_____

_____

_____

_____

_____

Now that you have removed some of the thoughts that clutter up your mind, try to sit for a moment or two and design your day.

You may wish to return to the thought that you caught and decide if it is something important or if it is a fear or? If it is something that will serve you, then write about it. What attention does it need? After you have completed this it is time to design your day:

1) What is most important for me today?

_____

_____

2) What do I need to do?

_____

_____

3) What are my goals for the day?

_____

_____

4) Who do I want to be today?

_____

_____

5) What do I need today?

_____

_____

Day 12 – Keep going! You're doing great!

Sit quietly. Breathe in 1, breathe out 2, in 3, out 4... relax. Breathe. Notice what your mind is doing. Is it mocking you? What stories is it telling you? Is it full of "shoulds" ? is it making fun of this practice or trying to sabotage your progress? Relax, breathe and just notice; don't judge. Just notice and accept that your mind is doing it's job; thinking.

After you have finished your "noticing meditation", catch a thought and write it down. Then dump all of the surrounding thoughts that don't serve you. Write.

_____

_____

_____

_____

_____

_____

_____

_____

_____

_____

_____

Now that you have removed some of the thoughts that clutter up your mind, try to sit for a moment or two and design your day.

You may wish to return to the thought that you caught and decide if it is something important or if it is a fear or? If it is something that will serve you, then write about it. What attention does it need? After you have completed this it is time to design your day:

1) What is most important for me today?

2) What do I need to do?

3) What are my goals for the day?

4) Who do I want to be today?

5) What do I need today?

Day 13 – You may not realize it now but you are preparing your self for a great life!

Sit quietly. Breathe in 1, breathe out 2, in 3, out 4... relax. Breathe. Notice what your mind is doing. Is it mocking you? What stories is it telling you? Is it full of "shoulds" ? is it making fun of this practice or trying to sabotage your progress? Relax, breathe and just notice; don't judge. Just notice and accept that your mind is doing it's job; thinking.

After you have finished your "noticing meditation", catch a thought and write it down. Then dump all of the surrounding thoughts that don't serve you. Write.

Now that you have removed some of the thoughts that clutter up your mind, try to sit for a moment or two and design your day.

You may wish to return to the thought that you caught and decide if it is something important or if it is a fear or? If it is something that will serve you, then write about it. What attention does it need? After you have completed this it is time to design your day:

1) What is most important for me today?

_____

_____

2) What do I need to do?

_____

_____

3) What are my goals for the day?

_____

_____

4) Who do I want to be today?

_____

_____

5) What do I need today?

_____

_____

Day 14 – Very often the only difference between success and failure is action!

Sit quietly. Breathe in 1, breathe out 2, in 3, out 4... relax. Breathe. Notice what your mind is doing. Is it mocking you? What stories is it telling you? Is it full of "shoulds" ? is it making fun of this practice or trying to sabotage your progress? Relax, breathe and just notice; don't judge. Just notice and accept that your mind is doing it's job; thinking.

After you have finished your "noticing meditation", catch a thought and write it down. Then dump all of the surrounding thoughts that don't serve you. Write.

☮

Now that you have removed some of the thoughts that clutter up your mind, try to sit for a moment or two and design your day.

You may wish to return to the thought that you caught and decide if it is something important or if it is a fear or? If it is something that will serve you, then write about it. What attention does it need? After you have completed this it is time to design your day:

1) What is most important for me today?

_____

_____

2) What do I need to do?

_____

_____

3) What are my goals for the day?

_____

_____

4) Who do I want to be today?

_____

_____

5) What do I need today?

_____

_____

Day 15

*You are half way through your first month of taking control of your mind and behavior. This is a great accomplishment and the rewards may be as simple as feeling calmer... Notice that this week there is an added topic to consider during your noticing meditation. It is going to safely have you begin a Spiritual exploration. Relax with it, have some fun with it... Ready for more? Now...

Do you feel like you are connecting to a Higher Power? What are your thoughts about a HP? Is this a difficult concept for you? You're not alone if it is. We will walk through this topic and you will gain in an idea or concept and learn to relax about it, let it grow or let it go. Don't worry, it will come. Breathe.

Sit quietly. Breathe in 1, breathe out 2, in 3, out 4... relax. Breathe. Notice what your mind is doing. Is it mocking you? What stories is it telling you? Is it full of "shoulds" ? is it making fun of this practice or trying to sabotage your progress? Relax, breathe and just notice; don't judge. Just notice and accept that your mind is doing it's job; thinking.

After you have finished your "noticing meditation", catch a thought and write it down. Then dump all of the surrounding thoughts that don't serve you. Write.

Now that you have removed some of the thoughts that clutter up your mind, try to sit for a moment or two and design your day.

You may wish to return to the thought that you caught and decide if it is something important or if it is a fear or? If it is something that will serve you, then write about it. What attention does it need? After you have completed this it is time to design your day:

1) What is most important for me today?

_____

_____

2) What do I need to do?

_____

_____

3) What are my goals for the day?

_____

_____

4) Who do I want to be today?

_____

_____

5) What do I need today?

_____

_____

Day 16

What are your thoughts about a HP today? Just breathe and considerate for a moment. Then ask the universe for an open mind and continue your practice. (If you already have a solid belief or religion, simply say thank you and ask for an open mind and heart). Breathe. Relax. It will happen.

Sit quietly. Breathe in 1, breathe out 2, in 3, out 4... relax. Breathe. Notice what your mind is doing. Is it mocking you? What stories is it telling you? Is it full of "shoulds" ? is it making fun of this practice or trying to sabotage your progress? Relax, breathe and just notice; don't judge. Just notice and accept that your mind is doing it's job; thinking.

After you have finished your "noticing meditation", catch a thought and write it down. Then dump all of the surrounding thoughts that don't serve you. Write.

_____

_____

_____

_____

_____

☮

_____

_____

_____

_____

_____

_____

_____

Now that you have removed some of the thoughts that clutter up your mind, try to sit for a moment or two and design your day.

You may wish to return to the thought that you caught and decide if it is something important or if it is a fear or? If it is something that will serve you, then write about it. What attention does it need? After you have completed this it is time to design your day:

1) What is most important for me today?

_____

_____

2) What do I need to do?

_____

_____

☮

3) What are my goals for the day?

_____

_____

4) Who do I want to be today?

_____

_____

5) What do I need today?

_____

_____

Day 17

Does using the name, "God" work for you or does it make you uncomfortable? If so, what will you call your HP? What are your thoughts about a HP today? Just breathe and considerate for a moment. Then ask the universe for an open mind and continue your practice. (If you already have a solid belief or religion, simply say thank you and ask for an open mind and heart)

Sit quietly. Breathe in 1, breathe out 2, in 3, out 4... relax. Breathe. Notice what your mind is doing. Is it mocking you? What stories is it telling you? Is it full of "shoulds" ? is it making fun of this practice or trying to sabotage your progress? Relax, breathe and just notice; don't judge. Just notice and accept that your mind is doing it's job; thinking.

After you have finished your "noticing meditation", catch a thought and write it down. Then dump all of the surrounding thoughts that don't serve you. Write.

_____

_____

_____

_____

_____

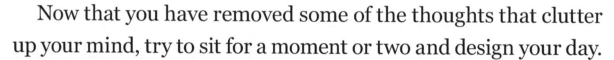

_____

_____

_____

_____

_____

_____

_____

Now that you have removed some of the thoughts that clutter up your mind, try to sit for a moment or two and design your day.

You may wish to return to the thought that you caught and decide if it is something important or if it is a fear or? If it is something that will serve you, then write about it. What attention does it need? After you have completed this it is time to design your day:

1) What is most important for me today?

_____

_____

2) What do I need to do?

_____

_____

☮

3) What are my goals for the day?

_____

_____

4) Who do I want to be today?

_____

_____

5) What do I need today?

_____

_____

49

Day 18

Are you feeling connected? What are your thoughts about a HP today? Just breathe and considerate for a moment. Then ask the universe for an open mind and continue your practice. (If you already have a solid belief or religion, simply say thank you and ask for an open mind and heart)

Sit quietly. Breathe in 1, breathe out 2, in 3, out 4… relax. Breathe. Notice what your mind is doing. Is it mocking you? What stories is it telling you? Is it full of "shoulds" ? is it making fun of this practice or trying to sabotage your progress? Relax, breathe and just notice; don't judge. Just notice and accept that your mind is doing it's job; thinking.

After you have finished your "noticing meditation", catch a thought and write it down. Then dump all of the surrounding thoughts that don't serve you. Write.

_____

_____

_____

_____

_____

☮

_____

_____

_____

_____

_____

_____

Now that you have removed some of the thoughts that clutter up your mind, try to sit for a moment or two and design your day.

You may wish to return to the thought that you caught and decide if it is something important or if it is a fear or? If it is something that will serve you, then write about it. What attention does it need? After you have completed this it is time to design your day:

1) What is most important for me today?

_____

_____

2) What do I need to do?

_____

_____

3) What are my goals for the day?

_____

_____

4) Who do I want to be today?

_____

_____

5) What do I need today?

_____

_____

Day 19

As you continue to explore your belief system, try just asking that it be revealed to you...

Now...

Sit quietly. Breathe in 1, breathe out 2, in 3, out 4... relax. Breathe. Notice what your mind is doing. Is it mocking you? What stories is it telling you? Is it full of "shoulds" ? is it making fun of this practice or trying to sabotage your progress? Relax, breathe and just notice; don't judge. Just notice and accept that your mind is doing it's job; thinking.

After you have finished your "noticing meditation", catch a thought and write it down. Then dump all of the surrounding thoughts that don't serve you. Write.

_____

_____

_____

_____

_____

Now that you have removed some of the thoughts that clutter up your mind, try to sit for a moment or two and design your day.

You may wish to return to the thought that you caught and decide if it is something important or if it is a fear or? If it is something that will serve you, then write about it. What attention does it need? After you have completed this it is time to design your day:

1) What is most important for me today?

_____

_____

2) What do I need to do?

_____

_____

3) What are my goals for the day?

_____

_____

☮

4) Who do I want to be today?

_____

_____

5) What do I need today?

_____

_____

Day 20

Are you feeling connected? What are your thoughts about a HP today? Just breathe and considerate for a moment. Then ask the universe for an open mind and continue your practice...

Sit quietly. Breathe in 1, breathe out 2, in 3, out 4... relax. Breathe. Notice what your mind is doing. Is it mocking you? What stories is it telling you? Is it full of "shoulds" ? is it making fun of this practice or trying to sabotage your progress? Relax, breathe and just notice; don't judge. Just notice and accept that your mind is doing it's job; thinking.

After you have finished your "noticing meditation", catch a thought and write it down. Then dump all of the surrounding thoughts that don't serve you. Write.

_____

_____

_____

_____

_____

_____

☮

_____

_____

_____

_____

_____

_____

Now that you have removed some of the thoughts that clutter up your mind, try to sit for a moment or two and design your day.

You may wish to return to the thought that you caught and decide if it is something important or if it is a fear or? If it is something that will serve you, then write about it. What attention does it need? After you have completed this it is time to design your day:

1) What is most important for me today?

_____

_____

2) What do I need to do?

_____

_____

3) What are my goals for the day?

_____

_____

4) Who do I want to be today?

_____

_____

5) What do I need today?

_____

_____

Day 21

How are you feeling about creating this new relationship with a creator? Are you able to relax with the concept yet? Just ask for it to be revealed... relax, breathe and begin your practice for the day.

Sit quietly. Breathe in 1, breathe out 2, in 3, out 4... relax. Breathe. Notice what your mind is doing. Is it mocking you? What stories is it telling you? Is it full of "shoulds" ? is it making fun of this practice or trying to sabotage your progress? Relax, breathe and just notice; don't judge. Just notice and accept that your mind is doing it's job; thinking.

After you have finished your "noticing meditation", catch a thought and write it down. Then dump all of the surrounding thoughts that don't serve you. Write.

_____

_____

_____

_____

_____

_____

(peace symbol)

_____

_____

_____

_____

_____

_____

_____

Now that you have removed some of the thoughts that clutter up your mind, try to sit for a moment or two and design your day.

You may wish to return to the thought that you caught and decide if it is something important or if it is a fear or? If it is something that will serve you, then write about it. What attention does it need? After you have completed this it is time to design your day:

1) What is most important for me today?

_____

_____

2) What do I need to do?

_____

_____

3) What are my goals for the day?

_____

_____

4) Who do I want to be today?

_____

_____

5) What do I need today?

_____

_____

Day 22

Continue to ask for it to be revealed and for a connection... relax, breathe and begin your practice for the day.

Sit quietly. Breathe in 1, breathe out 2, in 3, out 4... relax. Breathe. Notice what your mind is doing. Is it mocking you? What stories is it telling you? Is it full of "shoulds" ? is it making fun of this practice or trying to sabotage your progress? Relax, breathe and just notice; don't judge. Just notice and accept that your mind is doing it's job; thinking.

After you have finished your "noticing meditation", catch a thought and write it down. Then dump all of the surrounding thoughts that don't serve you. Write.

_____

_____

_____

_____

_____

_____

_____

_____

―――――――――――――――――――

―――――――――――――――――――

―――――――――――――――――――

―――――――――――――――――――

―――――――――――――――――――

Now that you have removed some of the thoughts that clutter up your mind, try to sit for a moment or two and design your day.

You may wish to return to the thought that you caught and decide if it is something important or if it is a fear or? If it is something that will serve you, then write about it. What attention does it need? After you have completed this it is time to design your day:

1) What is most important for me today?

―――――――――――――――――――

―――――――――――――――――――

2) What do I need to do?

―――――――――――――――――――

―――――――――――――――――――

3) What are my goals for the day?

―――――――――――――――――――

―――――――――――――――――――

☮

4) Who do I want to be today?

_____

_____

5) What do I need today?

_____

_____

Day 23

Is a Spiritual connection starting or do you feel frustrated? Go with it either way and just continue to ask; push through it! It will happen!

Sit quietly. Breathe in 1, breathe out 2, in 3, out 4... relax. Breathe. Notice what your mind is doing. Is it mocking you? What stories is it telling you? Is it full of "shoulds" ? is it making fun of this practice or trying to sabotage your progress? Relax, breathe and just notice; don't judge. Just notice and accept that your mind is doing it's job; thinking.

After you have finished your "noticing meditation", catch a thought and write it down. Then dump all of the surrounding thoughts that don't serve you. Write.

_____

_____

_____

_____

_____

_____

_____

_____

_____

_____

_____

_____

Now that you have removed some of the thoughts that clutter up your mind, try to sit for a moment or two and design your day.

You may wish to return to the thought that you caught and decide if it is something important or if it is a fear or? If it is something that will serve you, then write about it. What attention does it need? After you have completed this it is time to design your day:

1) What is most important for me today?

_____

_____

2) What do I need to do?

_____

_____

3) What are my goals for the day?

_____

_____

4) Who do I want to be today?

_____

_____

5) What do I need today?

_____

_____

Day 24

What is your name for your creator? Is it loving, kind, and forgiving?

Now...

Sit quietly. Breathe in 1, breathe out 2, in 3, out 4... relax. Breathe. Notice what your mind is doing. Is it mocking you? What stories is it telling you? Is it full of "shoulds" ? is it making fun of this practice or trying to sabotage your progress? Relax, breathe and just notice; don't judge. Just notice and accept that your mind is doing it's job; thinking.

After you have finished your "noticing meditation", catch a thought and write it down. Then dump all of the surrounding thoughts that don't serve you. Write.

_____

_____

_____

_____

_____

_____

_____

_____

☮

_____

_____

_____

_____

_____

Now that you have removed some of the thoughts that clutter up your mind, try to sit for a moment or two and design your day.

You may wish to return to the thought that you caught and decide if it is something important or if it is a fear or? If it is something that will serve you, then write about it. What attention does it need? After you have completed this it is time to design your day:

1) What is most important for me today?

_____

_____

2) What do I need to do?

_____

_____

3) What are my goals for the day?

_____

_____

4) Who do I want to be today?

_____

_____

5) What do I need today?

_____

_____

Day 25

Ask for guidance and practice trust...If it hasn't already, it will happen. Remain willing...

Now...

Sit quietly. Breathe in 1, breathe out 2, in 3, out 4... relax. Breathe. Notice what your mind is doing. Is it mocking you? What stories is it telling you? Is it full of "shoulds" ? is it making fun of this practice or trying to sabotage your progress? Relax, breathe and just notice; don't judge. Just notice and accept that your mind is doing it's job; thinking.

After you have finished your "noticing meditation", catch a thought and write it down. Then dump all of the surrounding thoughts that don't serve you. Write.

_____

_____

_____

_____

_____

_____

_____

_____

_____

_____

_____

_____

Now that you have removed some of the thoughts that clutter up your mind, try to sit for a moment or two and design your day.

You may wish to return to the thought that you caught and decide if it is something important or if it is a fear or? If it is something that will serve you, then write about it. What attention does it need? After you have completed this it is time to design your day:

1) What is most important for me today?

_____

_____

2) What do I need to do?

_____

_____

3) What are my goals for the day?

_____

_____

4) Who do I want to be today?

_____

_____

5) What do I need today?

_____

_____

Day 26

Are you open and willing? Great!!! What do you notice about your belief system now that you have practiced for a while?

Now...

Sit quietly. Breathe in 1, breathe out 2, in 3, out 4... relax. Breathe. Notice what your mind is doing. Is it mocking you? What stories is it telling you? Is it full of "shoulds" ? is it making fun of this practice or trying to sabotage your progress? Relax, breathe and just notice; don't judge. Just notice and accept that your mind is doing it's job; thinking.

After you have finished your "noticing meditation", catch a thought and write it down. Then dump all of the surrounding thoughts that don't serve you. Write.

_____

_____

_____

_____

_____

_____

_____

☮

_____

_____

_____

_____

_____

_____

Now that you have removed some of the thoughts that clutter up your mind, try to sit for a moment or two and design your day.

You may wish to return to the thought that you caught and decide if it is something important or if it is a fear or? If it is something that will serve you, then write about it. What attention does it need? After you have completed this it is time to design your day:

1) What is most important for me today?

_____

_____

2) What do I need to do?

_____

_____

3) What are my goals for the day?

_____

_____

☮

4) Who do I want to be today?

_____

_____

5) What do I need today?

_____

_____

Day 27

Do I feel like I am connecting to a Higher Power?

Now...

Sit quietly. Breathe in 1, breathe out 2, in 3, out 4... relax. Breathe. Notice what your mind is doing. Is it mocking you? What stories is it telling you? Is it full of "shoulds" ? is it making fun of this practice or trying to sabotage your progress? Relax, breathe and just notice; don't judge. Just notice and accept that your mind is doing it's job; thinking.

After you have finished your "noticing meditation", catch a thought and write it down. Then dump all of the surrounding thoughts that don't serve you. Write.

_____

_____

_____

_____

_____

Now that you have removed some of the thoughts that clutter up your mind, try to sit for a moment or two and design your day.

You may wish to return to the thought that you caught and decide if it is something important or if it is a fear or? If it is something that will serve you, then write about it. What attention does it need? After you have completed this it is time to design your day:

1) What is most important for me today?

_____

_____

2) What do I need to do?

_____

_____

3) What are my goals for the day?

_____

_____

4) Who do I want to be today?

_____

_____

5) What do I need today?

_____

_____

Day 28

Do I feel like I am connecting to a Higher Power? If so, what do you believe about this HP?

Now...

Sit quietly. Breathe in 1, breathe out 2, in 3, out 4... relax. Breathe. Notice what your mind is doing. Is it mocking you? What stories is it telling you? Is it full of "shoulds" ? is it making fun of this practice or trying to sabotage your progress? Relax, breathe and just notice; don't judge. Just notice and accept that your mind is doing it's job; thinking.

After you have finished your "noticing meditation", catch a thought and write it down. Then dump all of the surrounding thoughts that don't serve you. Write.

_____

_____

_____

_____

_____

_____

_____

☮

_____

_____

_____

_____

_____

Now that you have removed some of the thoughts that clutter up your mind, try to sit for a moment or two and design your day.

You may wish to return to the thought that you caught and decide if it is something important or if it is a fear or? If it is something that will serve you, then write about it. What attention does it need? After you have completed this it is time to design your day:

1) What is most important for me today?

_____

_____

2) What do I need to do?

_____

_____

3) What are my goals for the day?

_____

_____

4) Who do I want to be today?

_____

_____

5) What do I need today?

_____

_____

Day 29

Do I feel like I am connecting to a Higher Power? If so, what do you believe about this HP?

Now...

Sit quietly. Breathe in 1, breathe out 2, in 3, out 4... relax. Breathe. Notice what your mind is doing. Is it mocking you? What stories is it telling you? Is it full of "shoulds" ? is it making fun of this practice or trying to sabotage your progress? Relax, breathe and just notice; don't judge. Just notice and accept that your mind is doing it's job; thinking.

After you have finished your "noticing meditation", catch a thought and write it down. Then dump all of the surrounding thoughts that don't serve you. Write.

_____

_____

_____

_____

_____

Now that you have removed some of the thoughts that clutter up your mind, try to sit for a moment or two and design your day.

You may wish to return to the thought that you caught and decide if it is something important or if it is a fear or? If it is something that will serve you, then write about it. What attention does it need? After you have completed this it is time to design your day:

1) What is most important for me today?

_____

_____

2) What do I need to do?

_____

_____

3) What are my goals for the day?

_____

_____

4) Who do I want to be today?

_____

_____

5) What do I need today?

_____

_____

Day 30

Do I feel like I am connecting to a Higher Power? If so, what do you believe about this HP? You are almost done with your first month of Brain Dump, how do you feel?

What ways has this helped you? List here:

Now...

Sit quietly. Breathe in 1, breathe out 2, in 3, out 4... relax. Breathe. Notice what your mind is doing. Is it mocking you? What stories is it telling you? Is it full of "shoulds" ? Is it making fun of this practice or trying to sabotage your progress? Relax, breathe and *just notice*; *don't judge*. Just notice and accept that your mind is doing its job; *thinking*.

After you have finished your "noticing meditation", catch a thought and write it down. Then dump all of the surrounding thoughts that don't serve you. Write.

_____

_____

_____

_____

_____

_____

_____

_____

_____

_____

_____

Now that you have removed some of the thoughts that clutter up your mind, try to sit for a moment or two and design your day.

You may wish to return to the thought that you caught and decide if it is something important or if it is a fear or? If it is something that will serve you, then write about it. What attention does it need? After you have completed this it is time to design your day:

1) What is most important for me today?

_____

_____

2) What do I need to do?

_____

_____

3) What are my goals for the day?

_____

_____

4) Who do I want to be today?

_____

_____

5) What do I need today?

_____

_____

Day 31

Congratulations on taking your life in your own hands... What are more of the benefits that you notice in doing this practice?

Sitting quietly. Take few moments to reflect on your progress.

How have you changed? What benefits do you notice? How has your life changed? By now you have created a practice, your own personal practice.

You can, at this point, add a few minutes to your practice if that feels comfortable or you can continue to follow the path we have begun together, which ever feels best to you.

Breathe in 1, breathe out 2, in 3, out 4... relax. Breathe. Notice what your mind is doing. Is it mocking you? What stories is it telling you? Is it full of "shoulds" ? is it making fun of this practice or trying to sabotage your progress? Relax, breathe and just notice; don't judge. Just notice and accept that your mind is doing it's job; thinking.

After you have finished your "noticing meditation", catch a thought and write it down. Then dump all of the surrounding thoughts that don't serve you. Write.

_____

_____

_____

Now that you have removed some of the thoughts that clutter up your mind, try to sit for a moment or two and design your day.

You may wish to return to the thought that you caught and decide if it is something important or if it is a fear or? If it is something that will serve you, then write about it. What attention does it need? After you have completed this it is time to design your day:

1) What is most important for me today?

_____

_____

2) What do I need to do?

_____

_____

3) What are my goals for the day?

_____

_____

4) Who do I want to be today?

_____

_____

5) What do I need today?

_____

_____

This completes your first Brain Dump Journaling System, Brain Dump for New Recovery experience! You have a better understanding of you and you have added and aided to your recovery success. Enjoy

Look for future volumes addressing more issues such as romance, finance, and career/occupation.